CURSIVE HANDWRITING WORKBOOK FOR KIDS
Beginning Cursive

Welcome! **EXL Cursive Handwriting Workbooks** are designed to provide parents and teachers with fun and motivational tools for helping students master cursive handwriting.

Cursive Handwriting Workbook for Kids: Beginning Cursive helps children learn the basics of cursive writing in the most enjoyable and fun way! What makes this amazing workbook different from most other workbooks on beginning cursive, is that it provides **"dot to dot"- illustrated exercises** to help children understand how exactly to form each cursive letter and how to connect cursive letters. **In part 1**, students learn and practice the cursive alphabet. They have to draw the snail's trail inside the letter with a marker, following numbered dots, a fun way to learn how exactly to form each letter. Afterward, they practice writing the letter by tracing inside it and copying it multiple times. **In part 2**, students learn how to connect lowercase and uppercase cursive letters, and, **in part 3**, they practice writing their first words in cursive.

Important note: This workbook is the first book of our Cursive Handwriting Workbook Series. It is suitable for Grades 2 and up and it is meant to be used in the context of adult-guided lessons. Its purpose is to help children learn the cursive alphabet as well as to understand how to connect cursive letters and form short words in cursive. Upon finishing this workbook, students will be ready to move on to more advanced workbooks that will help them practice writing words and sentences with a goal to build fluency.

How Is This Workbook Organized?

The exercises in this workbook are divided into the following parts:

Can I Photocopy This Workbook?

This workbook is reproducible! Feel free to photocopy parts of it to use at work or home!

- Parents who purchase a copy of this workbook may reproduce worksheets for their family members.
- Teachers who purchase a copy of this workbook may reproduce worksheets for their classes. However, teachers are not allowed to reproduce worksheets for other teachers or an entire school. Please encourage other teachers to buy their own copies!

If you have questions or ideas on how we can improve this workbook, please feel free to contact Victoria Vita at hellovictoriavita@gmail.com

Concept and layout design by Victoria Vita. Credits to Ddraw and Freepik for some of the graphics used.

The Zaner-Bloser® style fonts used in producing this workbook can be purchased from Educational Fontware, Inc, www.educationalfontware.com. Special thanks to Mr. Dave Thompson of Educational Fontware, Inc for his kind support.

For questions, comments or ideas please contact: hellovictoriavita@gmail.com

ISBN-13: 978-1540695178

Part 1
The Cursive Alphabet
Learn and practice cursive letters a-z

Tips!

- **Use a light color marker or highlighter** to draw the snail trail! This way the numbered dots will remain visible afterwards and you can repeat the exercise as many times as you need!

- When tracing inside the letters, **use a soft B pencil or rollerball pen** instead of a ballpoint pen, for a more pleasant and smoother writing experience. Choose one in your favorite color!

- Don't forget to **tilt the page!** If you are right-handed, tilt the page so that the lower left corner of the page is closer to you. If you are left-handed, tilt the page so that the lower right corner is closer to you. This paper position facilitates proper letter slant in your handwriting.

- At the end of this workbook, you will find a blank lined page. Ask your parents or teacher to make copies of this page. Have these pages handy and use them when you need more writing space for extra practice.

| a | B | C | D | E | F | G | H | I | J | K | L | M | N | O | P | Q | R | S | T | U | V | W | X | Y | Z |
| a | b | c | d | e | f | g | h | i | j | k | l | m | n | o | p | q | r | s | t | u | v | w | x | y | z |

How to write cursive letter a

Draw the snail trail to learn how to write this letter.

With a light color marker, trace inside the letter by following the numbered dots.

Start at dot number 1!

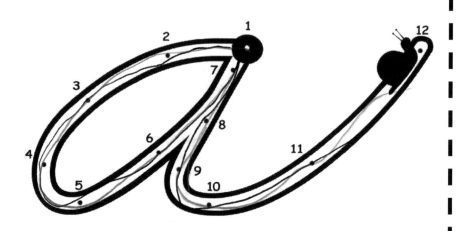

Let's practice! Trace inside the letter with a pen or pencil, then write it on your own!

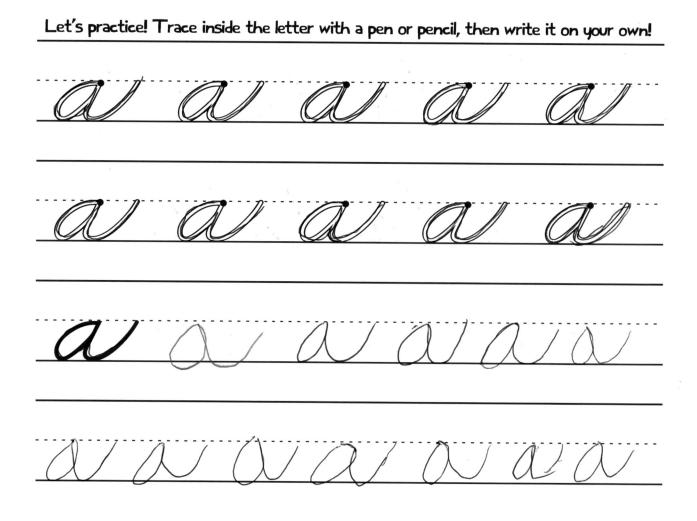

EXL

How to write cursive letter a

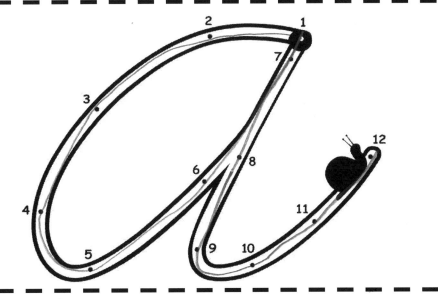

Draw the snail trail to learn how to write this letter.

With a light color marker, trace inside the letter by following the numbered dots.

Start at dot number 1!

Let's practice! Trace inside the letter with a pen or pencil, then write it on your own!

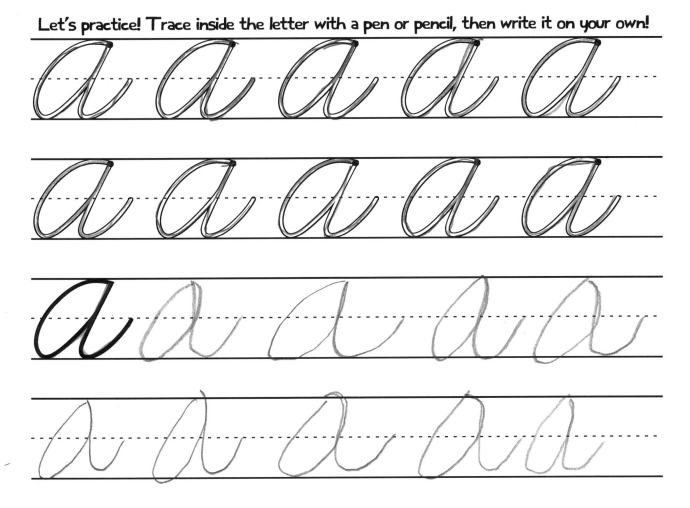

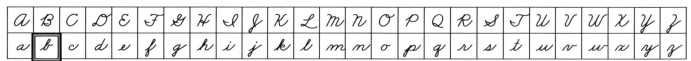

How to write cursive letter b

Draw the snail trail to learn how to write this letter.

With a light color marker, trace inside the letter by following the numbered dots.

Start at dot number 1!

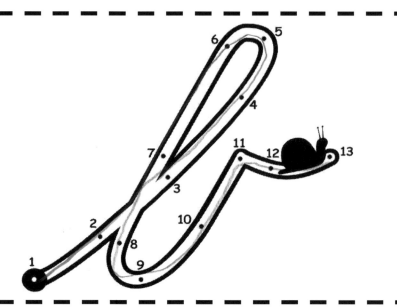

Let's practice! Trace inside the letter with a pen or pencil, then write it on your own!

How to write cursive letter

Draw the snail trail to learn how to write this letter.

With a light color marker, trace inside the letter by following the numbered dots.

Start at dot number 1!

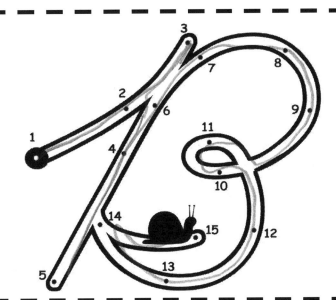

Let's practice! Trace inside the letter with a pen or pencil, then write it on your own!

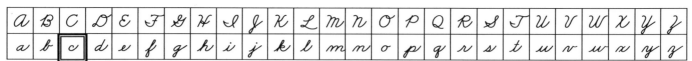

How to write cursive letter c

Draw the snail trail to learn how to write this letter.

With a light color marker, trace inside the letter by following the numbered dots.

Start at dot number 1!

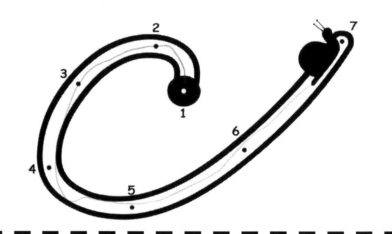

Let's practice! Trace inside the letter with a pen or pencil, then write it on your own!

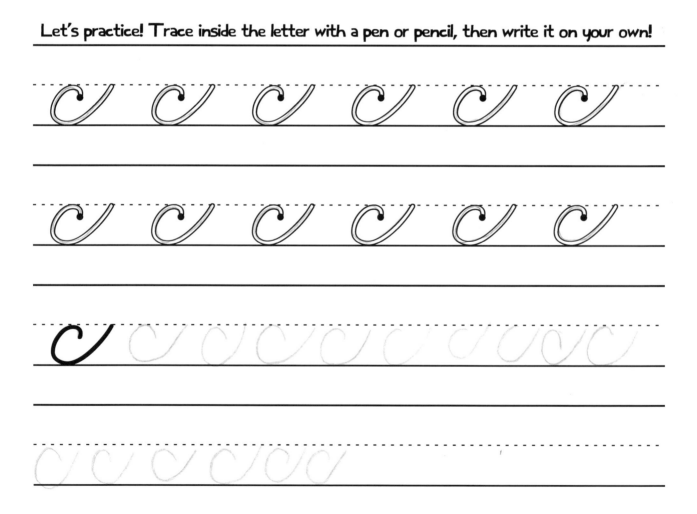

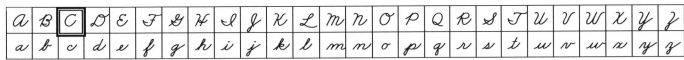

How to write cursive letter C

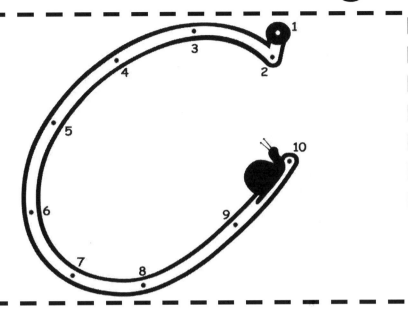

Draw the snail trail to learn how to write this letter.

With a light color marker, trace inside the letter by following the numbered dots.

Start at dot number 1!

Let's practice! Trace inside the letter with a pen or pencil, then write it on your own!

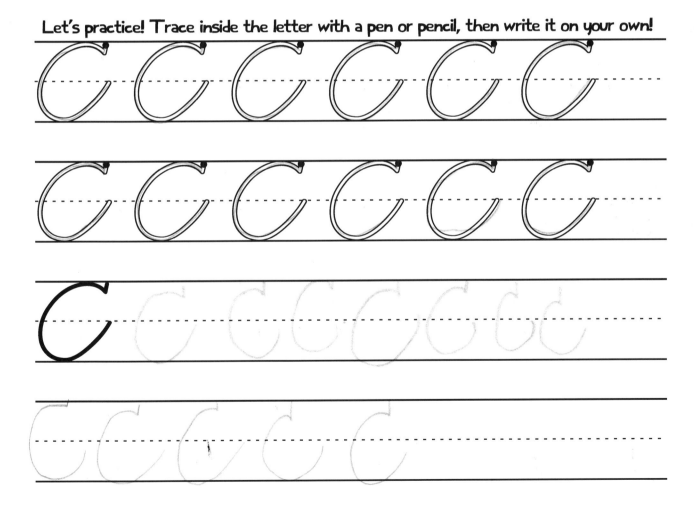

EXL

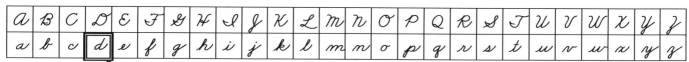

How to write cursive letter d

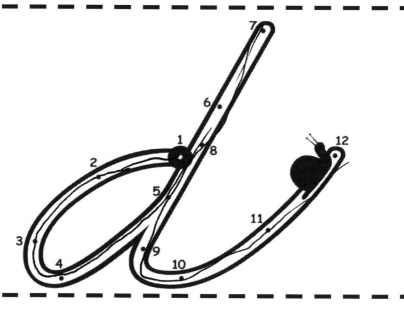

Draw the snail trail to learn how to write this letter.

With a light color marker, trace inside the letter by following the numbered dots.

Start at dot number 1!

Let's practice! Trace inside the letter with a pen or pencil, then write it on your own!

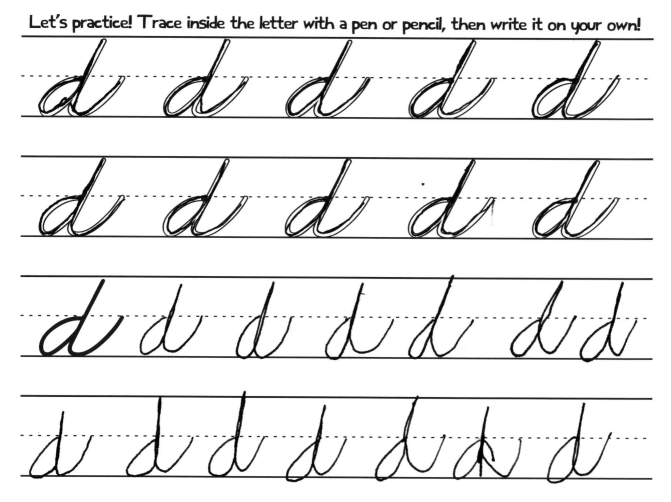

$\mathcal{A}$	$\mathcal{B}$	$\mathcal{C}$	$\mathcal{D}$	$\mathcal{E}$	$\mathcal{F}$	$\mathcal{G}$	$\mathcal{H}$	$\mathcal{I}$	$\mathcal{J}$	$\mathcal{K}$	$\mathcal{L}$	$\mathcal{M}$	$\mathcal{N}$	$\mathcal{O}$	$\mathcal{P}$	$\mathcal{Q}$	$\mathcal{R}$	$\mathcal{S}$	$\mathcal{T}$	$\mathcal{U}$	$\mathcal{V}$	$\mathcal{W}$	$\mathcal{X}$	$\mathcal{Y}$	$\mathcal{Z}$
a	b	c	d	e	f	g	h	i	j	k	l	m	n	o	p	q	r	s	t	u	v	w	x	y	z

How to write cursive letter $\mathcal{D}$

Draw the snail trail to learn how to write this letter.

With a light color marker, trace inside the letter by following the numbered dots.

Start at dot number 1!

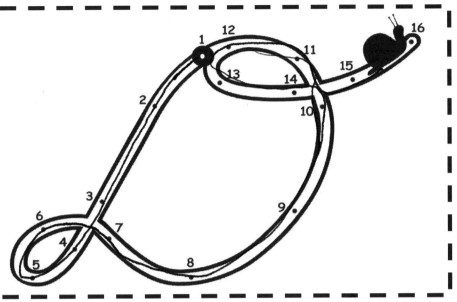

Let's practice! Trace inside the letter with a pen or pencil, then write it on your own!

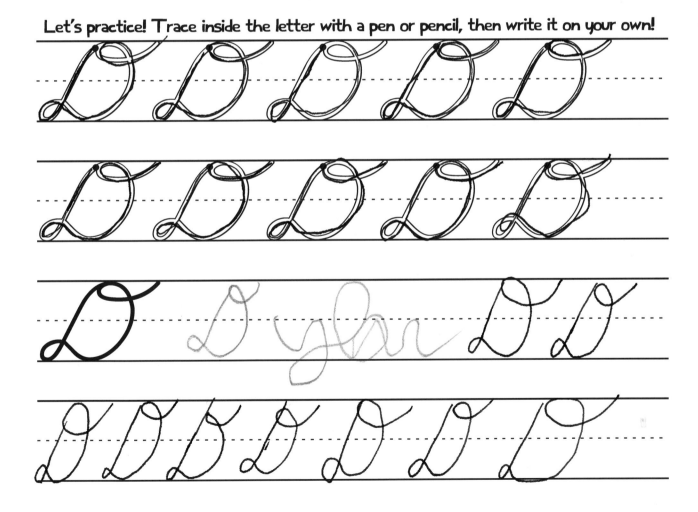

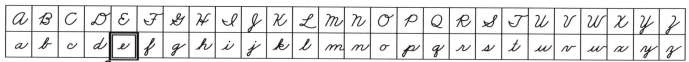

How to write cursive letter *e*

Draw the snail trail to learn how to write this letter.

With a light color marker, trace inside the letter by following the numbered dots.

Start at dot number 1!

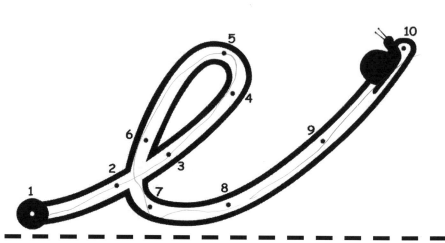

Let's practice! Trace inside the letter with a pen or pencil, then write it on your own!

ℓℓ ℓℓ ℓℓ ℓℓ ℓℓ ℓℓ

ℓℓ ℓℓ ℓℓ ℓℓ ℓℓ ℓℓ

ℓ ℓ ℓ ℓ ℓ ℓ ℓ ℓ ℓ

ℓ ℓ ℓ ℓ ℓ ℓ ℓ

Name:..
Cursive Handwriting Workbook for Kids: Beginning Cursive

How to write cursive letter $\mathcal{E}$

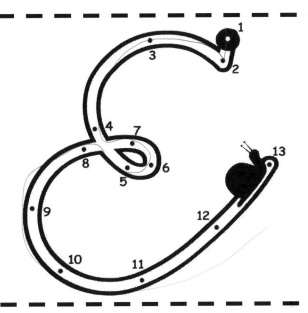

Draw the snail trail to learn how to write this letter.

With a light color marker, trace inside the letter by following the numbered dots.

Start at dot number 1!

Let's practice! Trace inside the letter with a pen or pencil, then write it on your own!

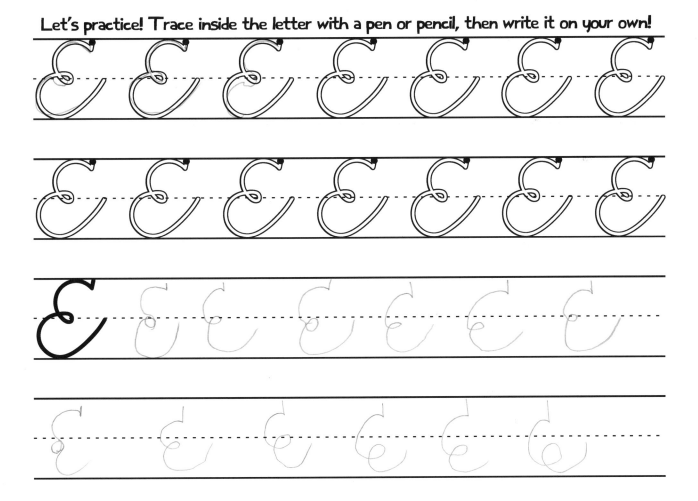

How to write cursive letter f

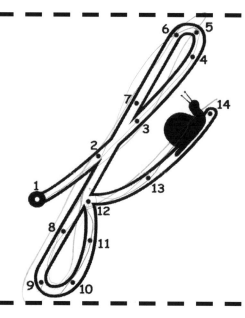

Draw the snail trail to learn how to write this letter.

With a light color marker, trace inside the letter by following the numbered dots.

Start at dot number 1!

Let's practice! Trace inside the letter with a pen or pencil, then write it on your own!

| $\mathcal{A}$ | $\mathcal{B}$ | $\mathcal{C}$ | $\mathcal{D}$ | $\mathcal{E}$ | **$\mathcal{F}$** | $\mathcal{G}$ | $\mathcal{H}$ | $\mathcal{I}$ | $\mathcal{J}$ | $\mathcal{K}$ | $\mathcal{L}$ | $\mathcal{M}$ | $\mathcal{N}$ | $\mathcal{O}$ | $\mathcal{P}$ | $\mathcal{Q}$ | $\mathcal{R}$ | $\mathcal{S}$ | $\mathcal{T}$ | $\mathcal{U}$ | $\mathcal{V}$ | $\mathcal{W}$ | $\mathcal{X}$ | $\mathcal{Y}$ | $\mathcal{Z}$ |
| a | b | c | d | e | f | g | h | i | j | k | l | m | n | o | p | q | r | s | t | u | v | w | x | y | z |

How to write cursive letter $\mathcal{F}$

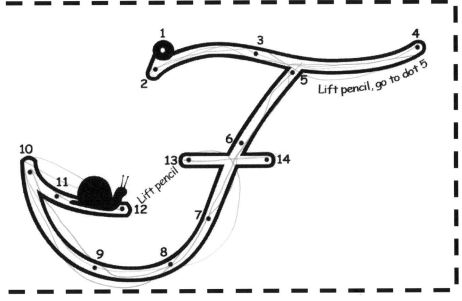

Draw the snail trail to learn how to write this letter.

With a light color marker, trace inside the letter by following the numbered dots.

Start at dot number 1!

Lift pencil, go to dot 5

Lift pencil

Let's practice! Trace inside the letter with a pen or pencil, then write it on your own!

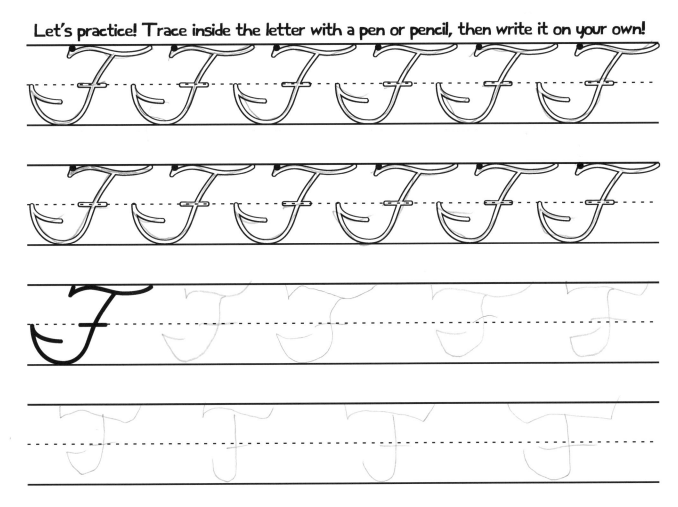

How to write cursive letter g

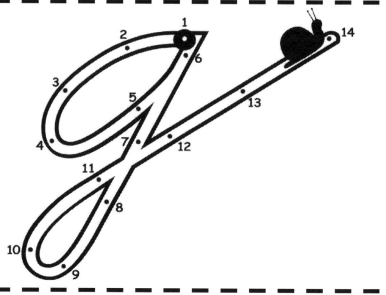

Draw the snail trail to learn how to write this letter.

With a light color marker, trace inside the letter by following the numbered dots.

Start at dot number 1!

Let's practice! Trace inside the letter with a pen or pencil, then write it on your own!

How to write cursive letter

Draw the snail trail to learn how to write this letter.

With a light color marker, trace inside the letter by following the numbered dots.

Start at dot number 1!

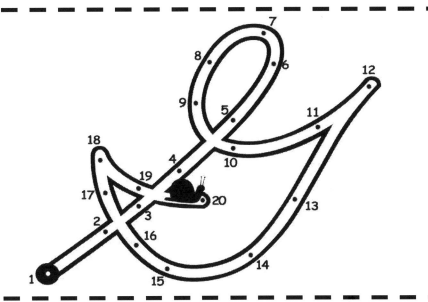

Let's practice! Trace inside the letter with a pen or pencil, then write it on your own!

$\mathcal{A}$	$\mathcal{B}$	$\mathcal{C}$	$\mathcal{D}$	$\mathcal{E}$	$\mathcal{F}$	$\mathcal{G}$	$\mathcal{H}$	$\mathcal{I}$	$\mathcal{J}$	$\mathcal{K}$	$\mathcal{L}$	$\mathcal{M}$	$\mathcal{N}$	$\mathcal{O}$	$\mathcal{P}$	$\mathcal{Q}$	$\mathcal{R}$	$\mathcal{S}$	$\mathcal{T}$	$\mathcal{U}$	$\mathcal{V}$	$\mathcal{W}$	$\mathcal{X}$	$\mathcal{Y}$	$\mathcal{Z}$
a	b	c	d	e	f	g	**h**	i	j	k	l	m	n	o	p	q	r	s	t	u	v	w	x	y	z

How to write cursive letter h

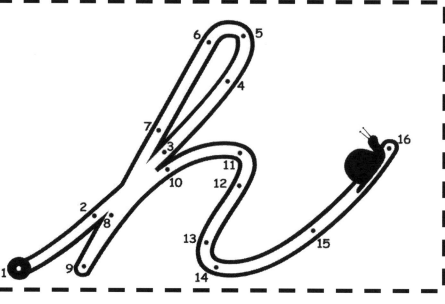

Draw the snail trail to learn how to write this letter.

With a light color marker, trace inside the letter by following the numbered dots.

Start at dot number 1!

Let's practice! Trace inside the letter with a pen or pencil, then write it on your own!

How to write cursive letter $\mathcal{H}$

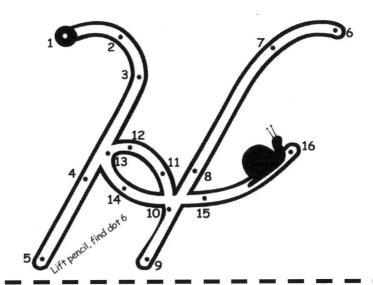

Draw the snail trail to learn how to write this letter.

With a light color marker, trace inside the letter by following the numbered dots.

Start at dot number 1!

Lift pencil, find dot 6

Let's practice! Trace inside the letter with a pen or pencil, then write it on your own!

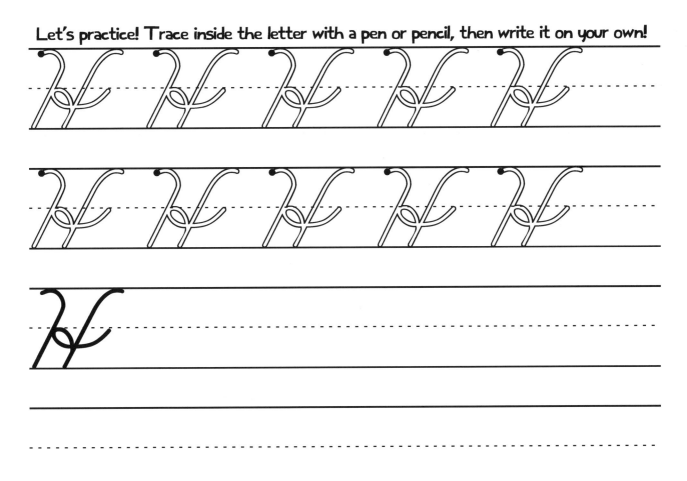

How to write cursive letter i

Draw the snail trail to learn how to write this letter.

With a light color marker, trace inside the letter by following the numbered dots.

Start at dot number 1!

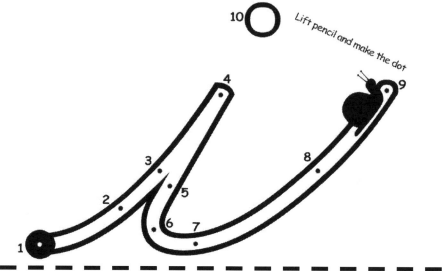

Lift pencil and make the dot

Let's practice! Trace inside the letter with a pen or pencil, then write it on your own!

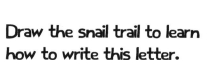

How to write cursive letter $\mathcal{l}$

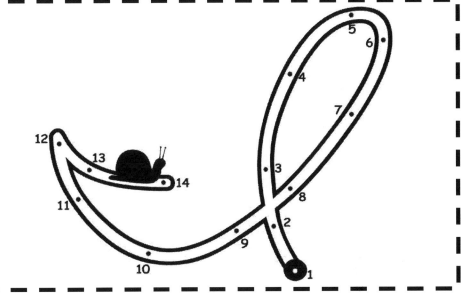

Draw the snail trail to learn how to write this letter.

With a light color marker, trace inside the letter by following the numbered dots.

Start at dot number 1!

Let's practice! Trace inside the letter with a pen or pencil, then write it on your own!

$\mathcal{A}$	$\mathcal{B}$	$\mathcal{C}$	$\mathcal{D}$	$\mathcal{E}$	$\mathcal{F}$	$\mathcal{G}$	$\mathcal{H}$	$\mathcal{I}$	$\mathcal{J}$	$\mathcal{K}$	$\mathcal{L}$	$\mathcal{M}$	$\mathcal{N}$	$\mathcal{O}$	$\mathcal{P}$	$\mathcal{Q}$	$\mathcal{R}$	$\mathcal{S}$	$\mathcal{T}$	$\mathcal{U}$	$\mathcal{V}$	$\mathcal{W}$	$\mathcal{X}$	$\mathcal{Y}$	$\mathcal{Z}$
a	b	c	d	e	f	g	h	i	j	k	l	m	n	o	p	q	r	s	t	u	v	w	x	y	z

How to write cursive letter j

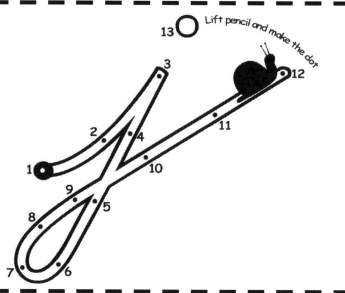

13 ◯ Lift pencil and make the dot

Draw the snail trail to learn how to write this letter.

With a light color marker, trace inside the letter by following the numbered dots.

Start at dot number 1!

Let's practice! Trace inside the letter with a pen or pencil, then write it on your own!

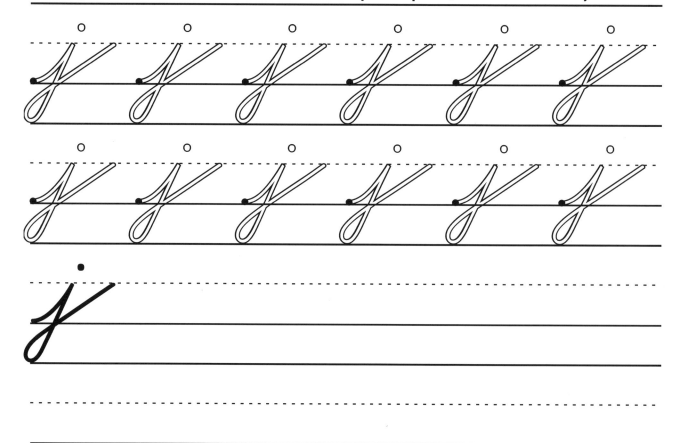

How to write cursive letter $\mathcal{L}$

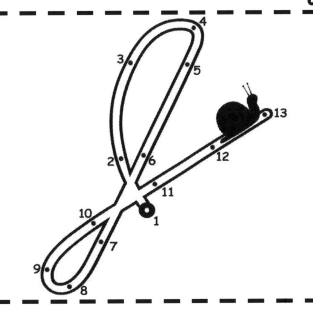

Draw the snail trail to learn how to write this letter.

With a light color marker, trace inside the letter by following the numbered dots.

Start at dot number 1!

Let's practice! Trace inside the letter with a pen or pencil, then write it on your own!

$\mathcal{A}$	$\mathcal{B}$	$\mathcal{C}$	$\mathcal{D}$	$\mathcal{E}$	$\mathcal{F}$	$\mathcal{G}$	$\mathcal{H}$	$\mathcal{I}$	$\mathcal{J}$	$\mathcal{K}$	$\mathcal{L}$	$\mathcal{M}$	$\mathcal{N}$	$\mathcal{O}$	$\mathcal{P}$	$\mathcal{Q}$	$\mathcal{R}$	$\mathcal{S}$	$\mathcal{T}$	$\mathcal{U}$	$\mathcal{V}$	$\mathcal{W}$	$\mathcal{X}$	$\mathcal{Y}$	$\mathcal{Z}$
a	b	c	d	e	f	g	h	i	j	k	l	m	n	o	p	r	s	t	u	v	w	x	y	z

How to write cursive letter k

Draw the snail trail to learn how to write this letter.

With a light color marker, trace inside the letter by following the numbered dots.

Start at dot number 1!

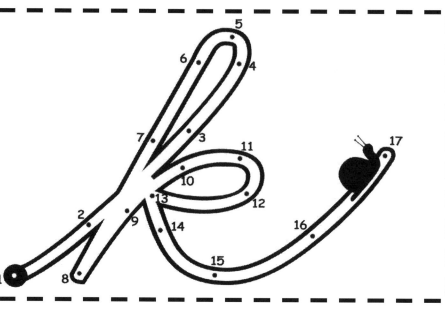

Let's practice! Trace inside the letter with a pen or pencil, then write it on your own!

k k k k k

k k k k k

k

How to write cursive letter K

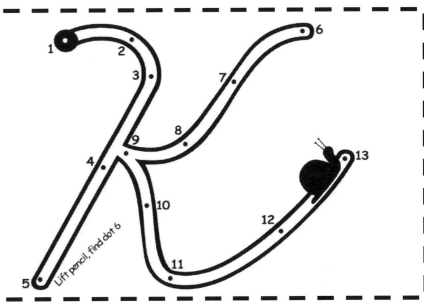

Draw the snail trail to learn how to write this letter.

With a light color marker, trace inside the letter by following the numbered dots.

Start at dot number 1!

Lift pencil, find dot 6

Let's practice! Trace inside the letter with a pen or pencil, then write it on your own!

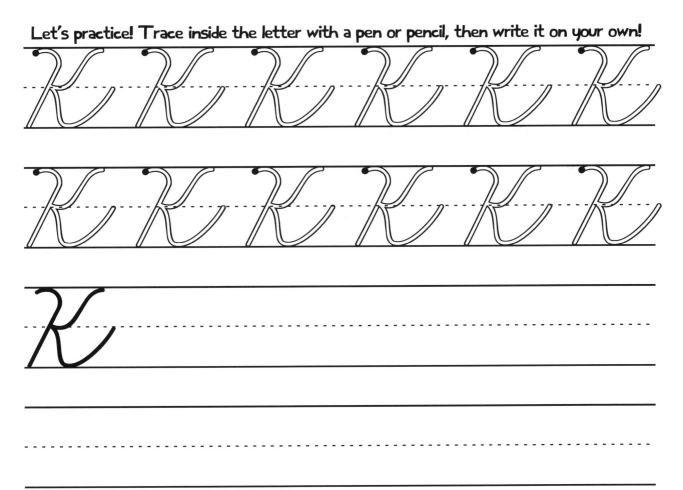

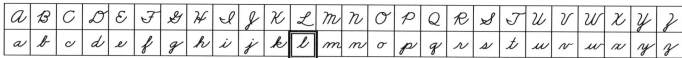

How to write cursive letter ℓ

Draw the snail trail to learn how to write this letter.

With a light color marker, trace inside the letter by following the numbered dots.

Start at dot number 1!

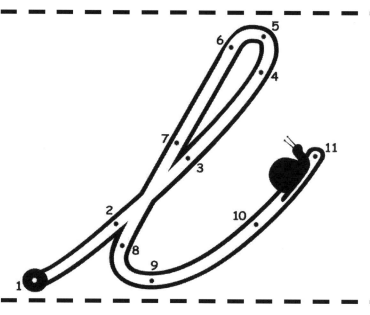

Let's practice! Trace inside the letter with a pen or pencil, then write it on your own!

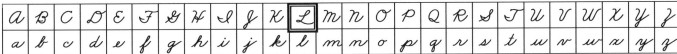

How to write cursive letter $\mathscr{L}$

Draw the snail trail to learn how to write this letter.

With a light color marker, trace inside the letter by following the numbered dots.

Start at dot number 1!

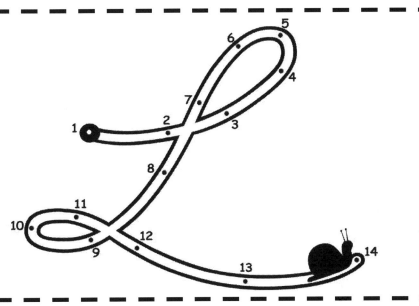

Let's practice! Trace inside the letter with a pen or pencil, then write it on your own!

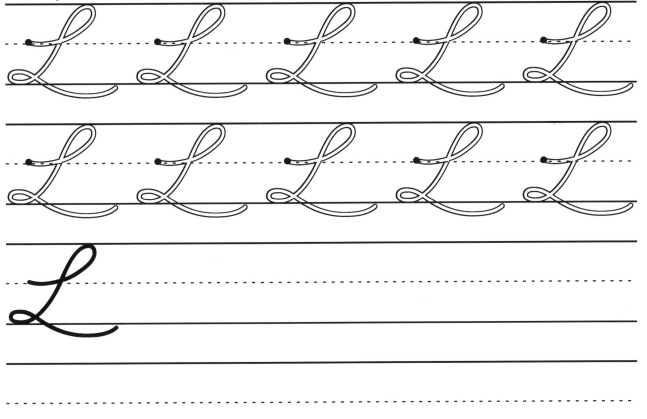

Name:...

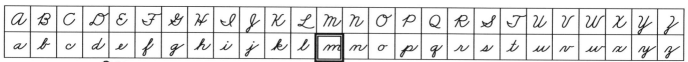

How to write cursive letter m

Draw the snail trail to learn how to write this letter.

With a light color marker, trace inside the letter by following the numbered dots.

Start at dot number 1!

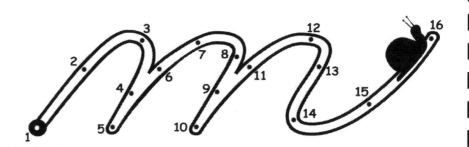

Let's practice! Trace inside the letter with a pen or pencil, then write it on your own!

How to write cursive letter m

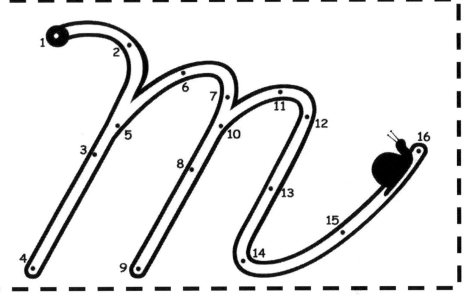

Draw the snail trail to learn how to write this letter.

With a light color marker, trace inside the letter by following the numbered dots.

Start at dot number 1!

Let's practice! Trace inside the letter with a pen or pencil, then write it on your own!

How to write cursive letter n

Draw the snail trail to learn how to write this letter.

With a light color marker, trace inside the letter by following the numbered dots.

Start at dot number 1!

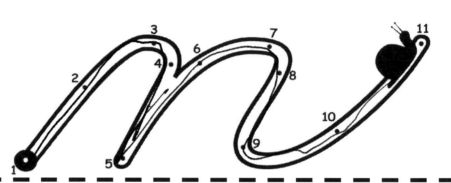

Let's practice! Trace inside the letter with a pen or pencil, then write it on your own!

How to write cursive letter n

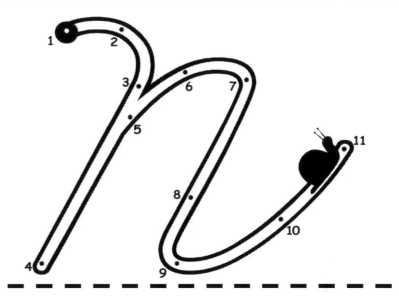

Draw the snail trail to learn how to write this letter.

With a light color marker, trace inside the letter by following the numbered dots.

Start at dot number 1!

Let's practice! Trace inside the letter with a pen or pencil, then write it on your own!

How to write cursive letter $\mathcal{O}$

Draw the snail trail to learn how to write this letter.

With a light color marker, trace inside the letter by following the numbered dots.

Start at dot number 1!

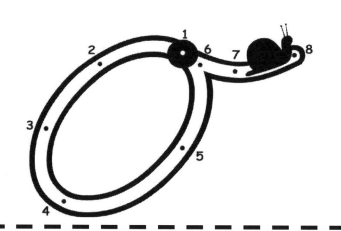

Let's practice! Trace inside the letter with a pen or pencil, then write it on your own!

$\mathcal{O}$ $\mathcal{O}$ $\mathcal{O}$ $\mathcal{O}$ $\mathcal{O}$ $\mathcal{O}$ $\mathcal{O}$

$\mathcal{O}$ $\mathcal{O}$ $\mathcal{O}$ $\mathcal{O}$ $\mathcal{O}$ $\mathcal{O}$ $\mathcal{O}$

$\mathcal{O}$

How to write cursive letter O

Draw the snail trail to learn how to write this letter.

With a light color marker, trace inside the letter by following the numbered dots.

Start at dot number 1!

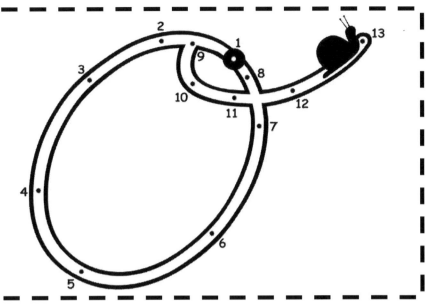

Let's practice! Trace inside the letter with a pen or pencil, then write it on your own!

How to write cursive letter p

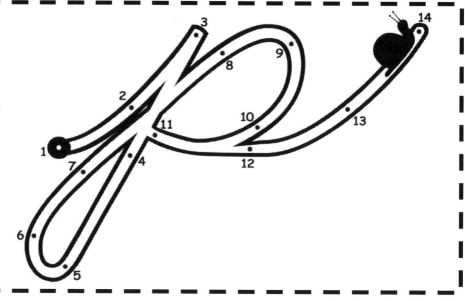

Draw the snail trail to learn how to write this letter.

With a light color marker, trace inside the letter by following the numbered dots.

Start at dot number 1!

Let's practice! Trace inside the letter with a pen or pencil, then write it on your own!

Name:...
Cursive Handwriting Workbook for Kids: Beginning Cursive

34

How to write cursive letter P

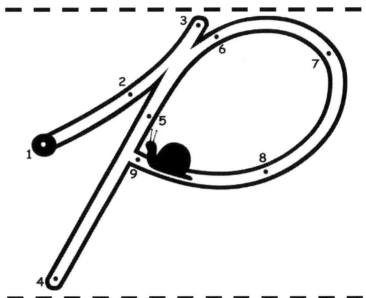

Draw the snail trail to learn how to write this letter.

With a light color marker, trace inside the letter by following the numbered dots.

Start at dot number 1!

Let's practice! Trace inside the letter with a pen or pencil, then write it on your own!

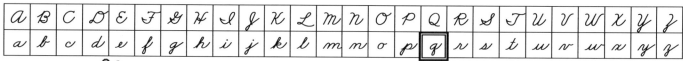

a	B	C	D	E	F	G	H	I	J	K	L	M	N	O	P	Q	R	S	T	U	V	W	X	Y	Z
a	b	c	d	e	f	g	h	i	j	k	l	m	n	o	p	q	r	s	t	u	v	w	x	y	z

How to write cursive letter q

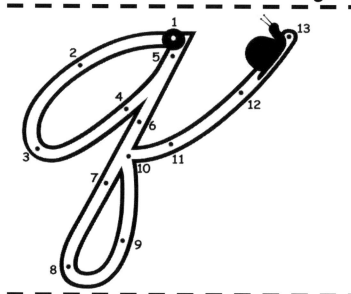

Draw the snail trail to learn how to write this letter.

With a light color marker, trace inside the letter by following the numbered dots.

Start at dot number 1!

Let's practice! Trace inside the letter with a pen or pencil, then write it on your own!

The Quick Brown Fox Jumped Over The Lazy Dog

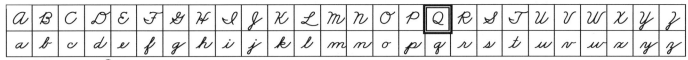

How to write cursive letter Q

Draw the snail trail to learn how to write this letter.

With a light color marker, trace inside the letter by following the numbered dots.

Start at dot number 1!

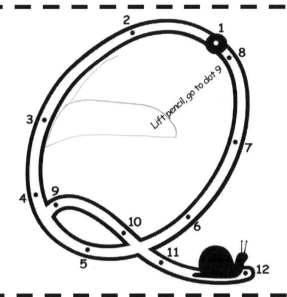

Lift pencil, go to dot 9

Let's practice! Trace inside the letter with a pen or pencil, then write it on your own!

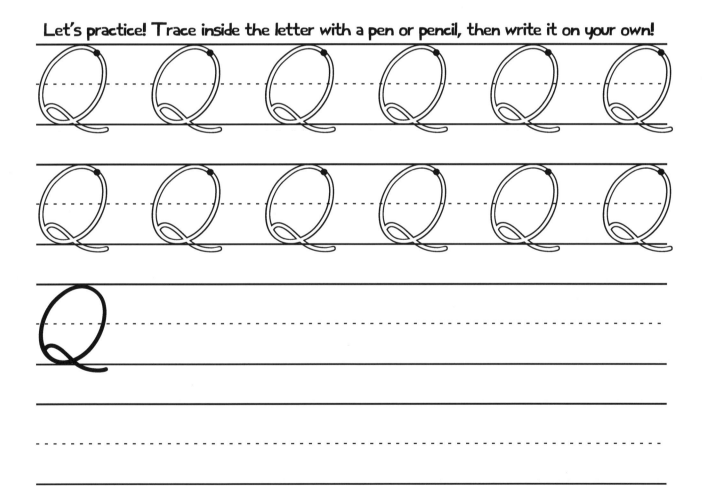

Name:...
Cursive Handwriting Workbook for Kids: Beginning Cursive

37

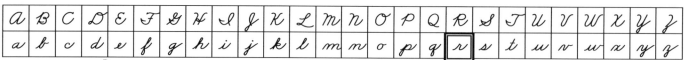

How to write cursive letter n

Draw the snail trail to learn how to write this letter.

With a light color marker, trace inside the letter by following the numbered dots.

Start at dot number 1!

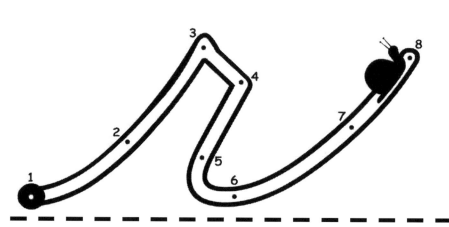

Let's practice! Trace inside the letter with a pen or pencil, then write it on your own!

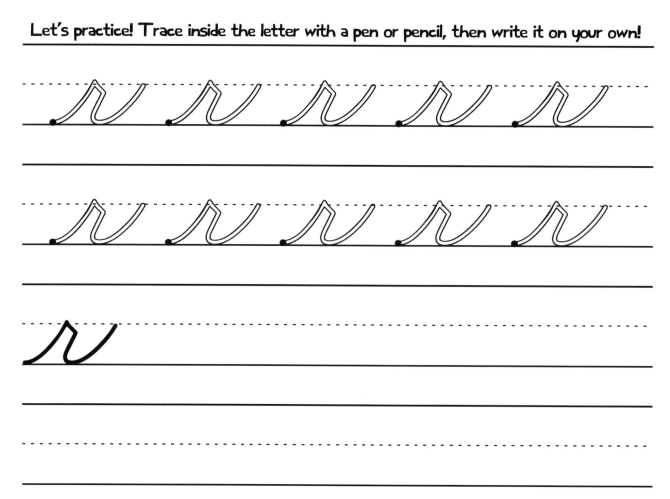

How to write cursive letter $\mathcal{R}$

Draw the snail trail to learn how to write this letter.

With a light color marker, trace inside the letter by following the numbered dots.

Start at dot number 1!

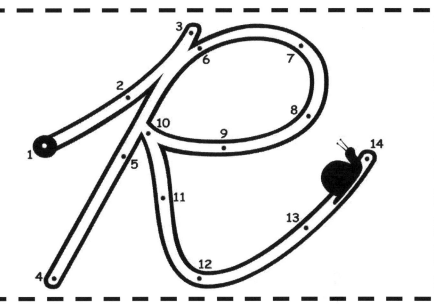

Let's practice! Trace inside the letter with a pen or pencil, then write it on your own!

How to write cursive letter s

Draw the snail trail to learn how to write this letter.

With a light color marker, trace inside the letter by following the numbered dots.

Start at dot number 1!

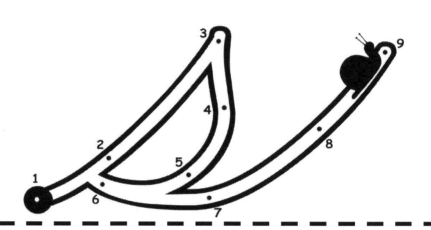

Let's practice! Trace inside the letter with a pen or pencil, then write it on your own!

EXL
Name:..
Cursive Handwriting Workbook for Kids: Beginning Cursive

40

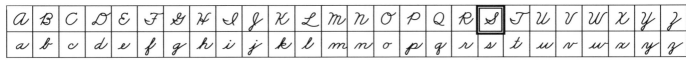

How to write cursive letter $\mathcal{S}$

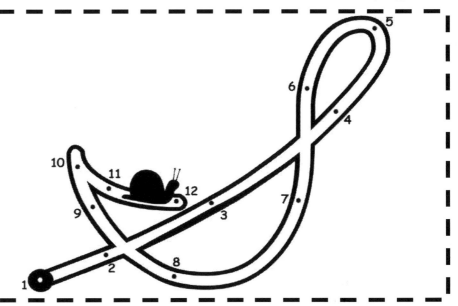

Draw the snail trail to learn how to write this letter.

With a light color marker, trace inside the letter by following the numbered dots.

Start at dot number 1!

Let's practice! Trace inside the letter with a pen or pencil, then write it on your own!

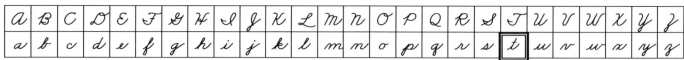

How to write cursive letter t

Draw the snail trail to learn how to write this letter.

With a light color marker, trace inside the letter by following the numbered dots.

Start at dot number 1!

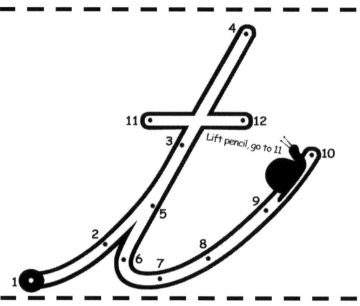

Lift pencil, go to 11

Let's practice! Trace inside the letter with a pen or pencil, then write it on your own!

t t t t t t

t t t t t t

t

How to write cursive letter $\mathcal{T}$

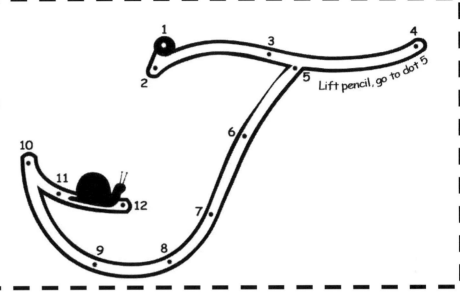

Draw the snail trail to learn how to write this letter.

With a light color marker, trace inside the letter by following the numbered dots.

Start at dot number 1!

Lift pencil, go to dot 5

Let's practice! Trace inside the letter with a pen or pencil, then write it on your own!

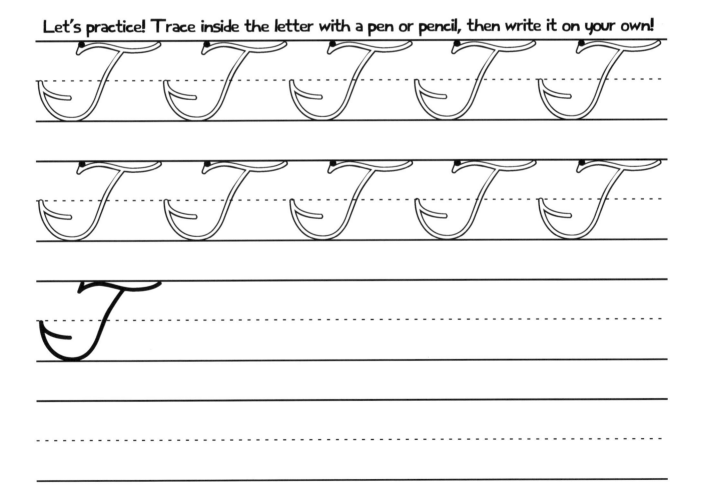

$\mathcal{A}$	$\mathcal{B}$	$\mathcal{C}$	$\mathcal{D}$	$\mathcal{E}$	$\mathcal{F}$	$\mathcal{G}$	$\mathcal{H}$	$\mathcal{I}$	$\mathcal{J}$	$\mathcal{K}$	$\mathcal{L}$	$\mathcal{M}$	$\mathcal{N}$	$\mathcal{O}$	$\mathcal{P}$	$\mathcal{Q}$	$\mathcal{R}$	$\mathcal{S}$	$\mathcal{T}$	$\mathcal{U}$	$\mathcal{V}$	$\mathcal{W}$	$\mathcal{X}$	$\mathcal{Y}$	$\mathcal{Z}$
a	b	c	d	e	f	g	h	i	j	k	l	m	n	o	p	q	r	s	t	u	v	w	x	y	z

How to write cursive letter w

Draw the snail trail to learn how to write this letter.

With a light color marker, trace inside the letter by following the numbered dots.

Start at dot number 1!

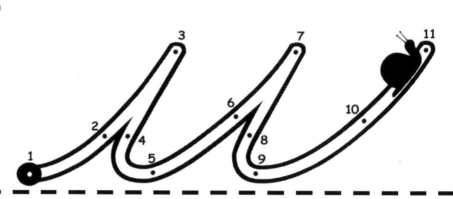

Let's practice! Trace inside the letter with a pen or pencil, then write it on your own!

$\mathcal{A}$	$\mathcal{B}$	$\mathcal{C}$	$\mathcal{D}$	$\mathcal{E}$	$\mathcal{F}$	$\mathcal{G}$	$\mathcal{H}$	$\mathcal{I}$	$\mathcal{J}$	$\mathcal{K}$	$\mathcal{L}$	$\mathcal{M}$	$\mathcal{N}$	$\mathcal{O}$	$\mathcal{P}$	$\mathcal{Q}$	$\mathcal{R}$	$\mathcal{S}$	$\mathcal{T}$	$\mathcal{U}$	$\mathcal{V}$	$\mathcal{W}$	$\mathcal{X}$	$\mathcal{Y}$	$\mathcal{Z}$
a	b	c	d	e	f	g	h	i	j	k	l	m	n	o	p	q	r	s	t	u	v	w	x	y	z

How to write cursive letter $\mathcal{U}$

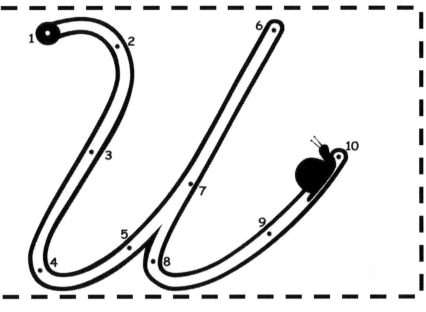

Draw the snail trail to learn how to write this letter.

With a light color marker, trace inside the letter by following the numbered dots.

Start at dot number 1!

Let's practice! Trace inside the letter with a pen or pencil, then write it on your own!

How to write cursive letter v

Draw the snail trail to learn how to write this letter.

With a light color marker, trace inside the letter by following the numbered dots.

Start at dot number 1!

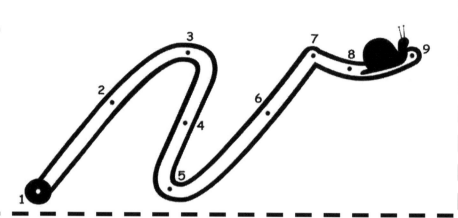

Let's practice! Trace inside the letter with a pen or pencil, then write it on your own!

| $\mathcal{A}$ | $\mathcal{B}$ | $\mathcal{C}$ | $\mathcal{D}$ | $\mathcal{E}$ | $\mathcal{F}$ | $\mathcal{G}$ | $\mathcal{H}$ | $\mathcal{I}$ | $\mathcal{J}$ | $\mathcal{K}$ | $\mathcal{L}$ | $\mathcal{M}$ | $\mathcal{N}$ | $\mathcal{O}$ | $\mathcal{P}$ | $\mathcal{Q}$ | $\mathcal{R}$ | $\mathcal{S}$ | $\mathcal{T}$ | $\mathcal{U}$ | $\mathcal{V}$ | $\mathcal{W}$ | $\mathcal{X}$ | $\mathcal{Y}$ | $\mathcal{Z}$ |
| a | b | c | d | e | f | g | h | i | j | k | l | m | n | o | p | q | r | s | t | u | v | w | x | y | z |

How to write cursive letter $\mathcal{V}$

Draw the snail trail to learn how to write this letter.

With a light color marker, trace inside the letter by following the numbered dots.

Start at dot number 1!

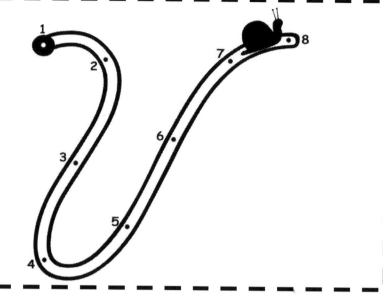

Let's practice! Trace inside the letter with a pen or pencil, then write it on your own!

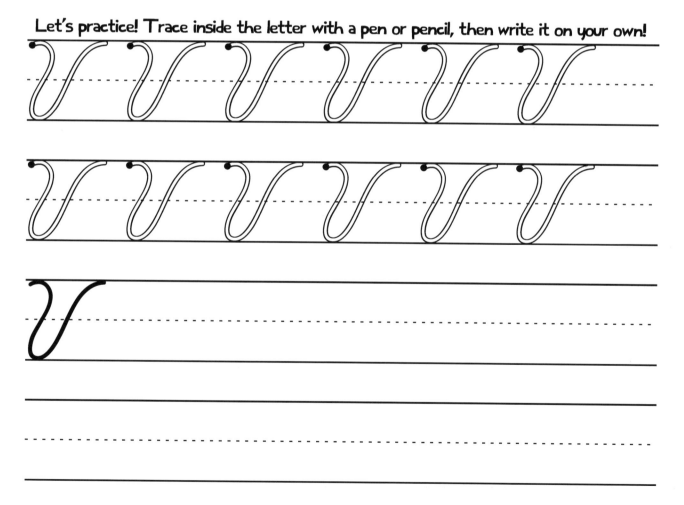

How to write cursive letter w

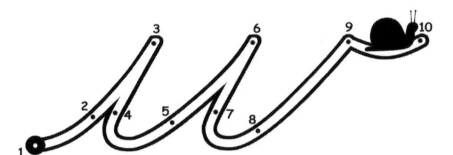

Draw the snail trail to learn how to write this letter.

With a light color marker, trace inside the letter by following the numbered dots.

Start at dot number 1!

Let's practice! Trace inside the letter with a pen or pencil, then write it on your own!

How to write cursive letter *W*

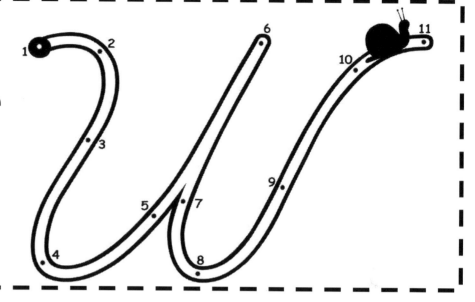

Draw the snail trail to learn how to write this letter.

With a light color marker, trace inside the letter by following the numbered dots.

Start at dot number 1!

Let's practice! Trace inside the letter with a pen or pencil, then write it on your own!

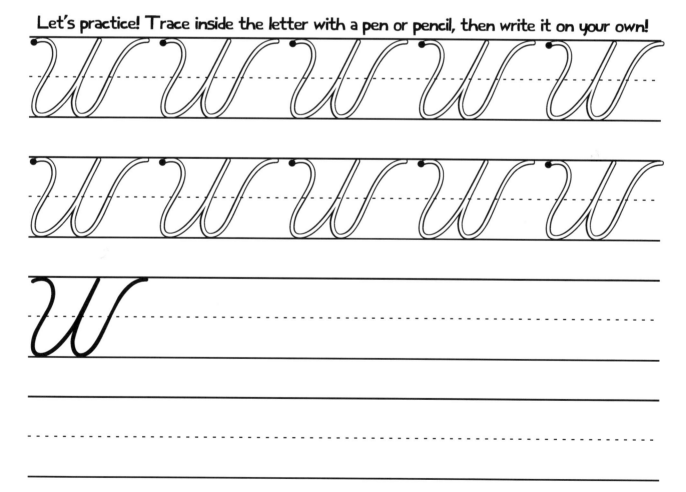

How to write cursive letter x

Draw the snail trail to learn how to write this letter.

With a light color marker, trace inside the letter by following the numbered dots.

Start at dot number 1!

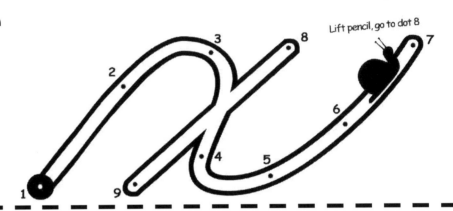

Lift pencil, go to dot 8

Let's practice! Trace inside the letter with a pen or pencil, then write it on your own!

EXL

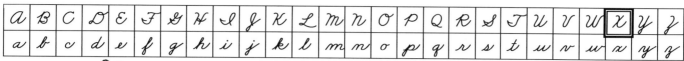

How to write cursive letter $\mathcal{X}$

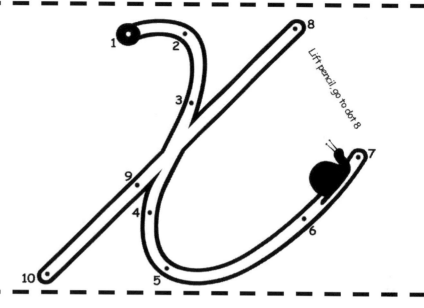

Draw the snail trail to learn how to write this letter.

With a light color marker, trace inside the letter by following the numbered dots.

Start at dot number 1!

Lift pencil, go to dot 8

Let's practice! Trace inside the letter with a pen or pencil, then write it on your own!

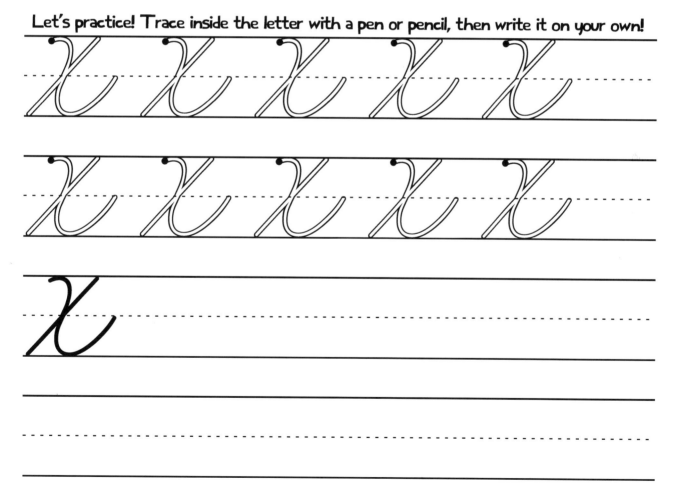

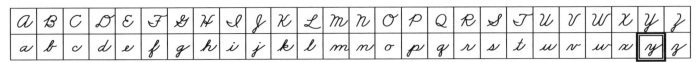

How to write cursive letter $\mathcal{Y}$

Draw the snail trail to learn how to write this letter.

With a light color marker, trace inside the letter by following the numbered dots.

Start at dot number 1!

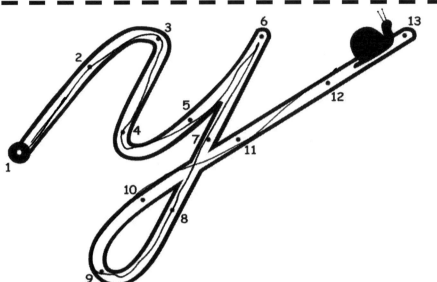

Let's practice! Trace inside the letter with a pen or pencil, then write it on your own!

How to write cursive letter $\mathcal{Y}$

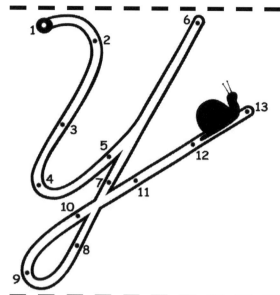

Draw the snail trail to learn how to write this letter.

With a light color marker, trace inside the letter by following the numbered dots.

Start at dot number 1!

Let's practice! Trace inside the letter with a pen or pencil, then write it on your own!

How to write cursive letter

Draw the snail trail to learn how to write this letter.

With a light color marker, trace inside the letter by following the numbered dots.

Start at dot number 1!

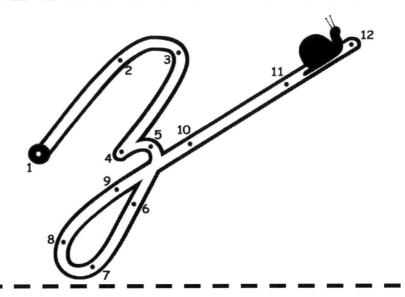

Let's practice! Trace inside the letter with a pen or pencil, then write it on your own!

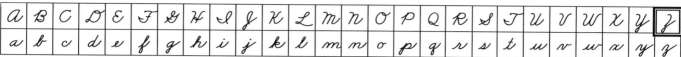

| a | B | C | D | E | F | G | H | I | J | K | L | M | N | O | P | Q | R | S | T | U | V | W | X | Y | Z |
| a | b | c | d | e | f | g | h | i | j | k | l | m | n | o | p | q | r | s | t | u | v | w | x | y | z |

How to write cursive letter $\mathcal{Z}$

Draw the snail trail to learn how to write this letter.

With a light color marker, trace inside the letter by following the numbered dots.

Start at dot number 1!

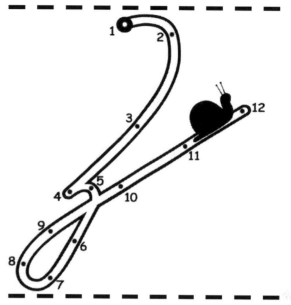

Let's practice! Trace inside the letter with a pen or pencil, then write it on your own!

Test: How many cursive letters can you remember?

What animal do you see? Write the letters in cursive.

1   2   3

1   2   3

1   2   3

1   2   3

1   2   3   4

1   2   3   4

1   2   3   4   5

1   2   3   4   5

Part 2
Connecting Letters
Learn how to connect cursive letters

Tips!

- **Use a light color marker or highlighter** to draw the snail trail in the warm-up exercises! This way the numbered dots will remain visible afterwards and you can repeat the exercise as many times as you need!

- When tracing inside the letters, **use a soft B pencil or rollerball pen** instead of a ballpoint pen, for a more pleasant and smoother writing experience. Choose one in your favorite color!

- Don't forget to **tilt the page!** If you are right-handed, tilt the page so that the lower left corner of the page is closer to you. If you are left-handed, tilt the page so that the lower right corner is closer to you. This paper position facilitates proper letter slant in your handwriting.

- At the end of this workbook, you will find a blank lined page. Ask your parents or teacher to make copies of this page. Have these pages handy and use them when you need more writing space for extra practice.

Warm-up exercises

Draw the snail trail to learn how to connect two cursive letters! On this page there are three examples (aa, at, ad). With a light color marker, trace inside the letters by following the numbered dots.

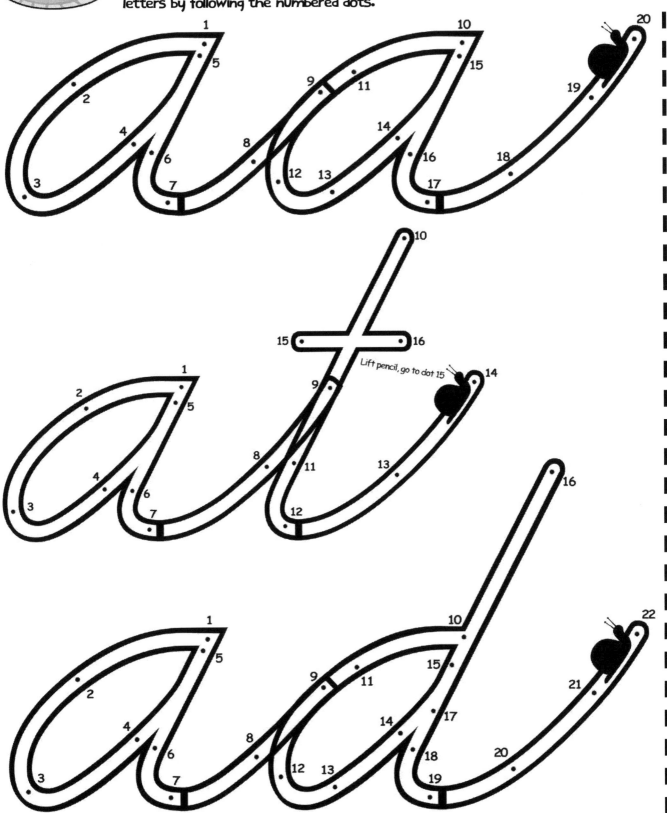

Lift pencil, go to dot 15

Name:...
Cursive Handwriting Workbook for Kids: Beginning Cursive

58

Warm-up exercises

Let's see four more examples (cc, co, dd, gg). With a light color marker, trace inside the letters by following the numbered dots. When you finish, go to the next page.

Name: ....
Cursive Handwriting Workbook for Kids: Beginning Cursive

59

How to connect cursive letter *a*

Trace inside the letters with a pen or pencil, then finish the line by repeating the letters!

a a aa aa aa

aa

a d ad ad ad

ad

a t at at at at

at

a n an an an

an

How to connect cursive letter

Trace inside the letters with a pen or pencil, then finish the line by repeating the letters!

bb bb bb bb bb

bb

b a ba ba ba

ba

be be be be be

be

br br br br br

br

How to connect cursive letter *c*

Trace inside the letters with a pen or pencil, then finish the line by repeating the letters!

c c cc cc cc cc

cc

ca ca ca ca ca

ca

co co co co co co

co

cr cr cr cr cr cr

cr

Name:...
Cursive Handwriting Workbook for Kids: Beginning Cursive

62

How to connect cursive letter d

Trace inside the letters with a pen or pencil, then finish the line by repeating the letters!

d   d   dd   dd   dd

dd

d o   do   do   do   do

do

d a   da   da   da

da

d i   di   di   di   di   di

di

How to connect cursive letter *e*

Trace inside the letters with a pen or pencil, then finish the line by repeating the letters!

e e ee ee ee ee

ee

e g eg eg eg eg

eg

e d ed ed ed ed

ed

em em em em

em

How to connect cursive letter f

Trace inside the letters with a pen or pencil, then finish the line by repeating the letters!

ff ff ff ff ff ff ff

ff

fo fo fo fo fo fo fo

fo

fw fw fw fw fw

fw

fr fr fr fr fr

fr

How to connect cursive letters g, h

Trace inside the letters with a pen or pencil, then finish the line by repeating the letters!

g g g gg h h h hh

gg

hh

g o o go go go go go

go

g r r gr gr gr gr gr

gr

hi hi hi hi hi

hi

How to connect cursive letters i, j

Trace inside the letters with a pen or pencil, then finish the line by repeating the letters!

ii

jj

it

it

if

if

jo

jo

Name: ....

Cursive Handwriting Workbook for Kids: Beginning Cursive

How to connect cursive letters *k , l*

Trace inside the letters with a pen or pencil, then finish the line by repeating the letters!

k   k   k   kk   kk   ll   ll   ll

kk

ll

ke   ke   ke   ke   ke   ke

ke

kn   kn   kn   kn   kn

kn

lo   lo   lo   lo   lo   lo   lo

lo

Name:..
Cursive Handwriting Workbook for Kids: Beginning Cursive

EXL

68

How to connect cursive letters m, n

Trace inside the letters with a pen or pencil, then finish the line by repeating the letters!

m m m m m m m m m

m m m

n n n n n n n n

n n n

m a m a m a

m a

n o n o n o n o

n o

How to connect cursive letters *o, p*

Trace inside the letters with a pen or pencil, then finish the line by repeating the letters!

o o oo p p pp

oo

pp

on on on on

on

of of of of of of

of

pr pr pr pr

pr

Name:...
Cursive Handwriting Workbook for Kids: Beginning Cursive

70

How to connect cursive letters q , r

Trace inside the letters with a pen or pencil, then finish the line by repeating the letters!

q q q qq r r rr

qq

rr

r a ra ra ra

ra

r t rt rt rt rt

rt

q u qu qu qu

qu

Name:...

Cursive Handwriting Workbook for Kids: Beginning Cursive

How to connect cursive letters *s,t*

Trace inside the letters with a pen or pencil, then finish the line by repeating the letters!

s s s ss ss t t tt

ss

tt

sk sk sk sk

sk

sp sp sp sp

sp

to to to to to

to

How to connect cursive letters *uu , n*

Trace inside the letters with a pen or pencil, then finish the line by repeating the letters!

uu uu uuuu n n nn

uuu

nn

uun uun uun uun

uun

us us us us

us

nn nn nn nn

ni

How to connect cursive letters *w , x*

Trace inside the letters with a pen or pencil, then finish the line by repeating the letters!

ww ww ww ww

ww

xx xx xx xx

xx

we we we we

we

xy xy xy xy

xy

How to connect cursive letters *y , z*

Trace inside the letters with a pen or pencil, then finish the line by repeating the letters!

yy yy yy zz zz zz

yy

zz

ye ye ye ye ye

ye

yo yo yo yo yo

yo

zi zi zi zi zi

zi

Connecting uppercase cursive letters

These uppercase letters connect to lowercase letters: A,C,E,H,J,K,M,N,R,U,X,Y,Z

Ant

Bee

Cat

Dog

Egg

Fox

Gym

Hen

Ice

Name:..
Cursive Handwriting Workbook for Kids: Beginning Cursive

76

Connecting uppercase cursive letters

These uppercase letters connect to lowercase letters: A,C,E,H,J,K,M,N,R,U,X,Y,Z

Jam

Key

Leg

Map

Net

Owl

Pig

Quiz

Rat

Connecting uppercase cursive letters

These uppercase letters connect to lowercase letters: A,C,E,H,J,K,M,N,R,U,X,Y,Z

Sky

Tea

Ufo

Vase

Wax

Xmas

You

Zoo

Part 3
Advanced Practice
Writing my first words in cursive

Tips!

- **Use a soft B pencil or rollerball pen**!
- Don't forget to **tilt the page!**
- When tracing or writing words, wait until all letters in a word are formed before going back to add any dots or crosses.
- This last part is only an introduction to writing words in cursive. Having completed this workbook on beginning cursive (Level 1), the next step is to further practice writing words in cursive (Level 2) and finally, practice writing sentences in cursive (Level 3). When you finish this workbook, you will be ready to move on to more advanced workbooks that will help you practice writing words and sentences in cursive, improve your fluency and refine your writing.

Name:...
Cursive Handwriting Workbook for Kids: Beginning Cursive

79

Writing my first words in cursive

First trace inside the letters, then write the word on your own!

cat cat cat

dog dog dog

pig pig pig

fox fox fox

bee bee bee

Writing my first words in cursive

First trace inside the letters, then write the word on your own!

box box box

egg egg egg

hat hat hat

ball ball ball

cow cow cow

Writing my first words in cursive

First trace inside the letters, then write the word on your own!

boy boy boy

girl girl girl

man man man

book book book

pen pen pen

Writing my first words in cursive

First trace inside the letters, then write the word on your own!

one one one

two two two

three three three

four four four

five five five

Name: ....
Cursive Handwriting Workbook for Kids: Beginning Cursive

83

Writing my first words in cursive

First trace inside the letters, then write the word on your own!

red red red

blue blue blue

big big big

good good good

old old old

Name:..
Cursive Handwriting Workbook for Kids: Beginning Cursive

84

Writing my first words in cursive

First trace inside the letters, then write the word on your own!

sit sit sit

run run run

eat eat eat

play play play

sleep sleep sleep

Name:..
Cursive Handwriting Workbook for Kids: Beginning Cursive

85

Writing my first words in cursive

First trace inside the letters, then write the word on your own!

mom mom mom

dad dad dad

home home home

love love love

fun fun fun

Writing my first words in cursive

First trace inside the letters, then write the words on your own!

I am happy!

I can now write

in cursive!

Cursive writing

is fun!

Hi!

My name is Victoria Vita.
My team I worked hard to create this workbook!
If you enjoyed it and found it useful,
please ask your mom or dad to help you
write a review on Amazon!
Your kind reviews and honest comments
will encourage us
to keep making more books like this!
Thank you!

Victoria Vita

Ps. If you have comments or ideas on how we can improve
this workbook, feel free to contact me
at my personal email: hellovictoriavita@gmail.com

Made in the USA
San Bernardino, CA
20 October 2017